10 CHRISTMAS VOL. 4

MW00902109

CONTENTS

ARRANGEMENTS BY B. C. DOCKERY ©2022

Angels From the Realm of Glory

Henry Smar
B. C. Dockery

Arr. ©2022

Coventry Carol

Traditiona
B. C. Dockery

Gesu Bambino

Pietro Yon
B. C. Dockery

Arr. ©2022

Gesu Bambino

Good Christian Men, Rejoice!

Traditional German

B. C. Dockery

Lo, How a Rose E'er Blooming

Traditional
B. C. Dockery

Arr. ©2022

O Christmas Tree

O Tannenbaum

Traditional German

B. C. Dockery

The Holly and the Ivy

Traditional English
B. C. Dockery

Vln.

Vln.

Up on the Housetop

Benjamin Hanby
B. C. Dockery

Arr. ©2022

Here We Come A-Caroling

Wassail Song

Traditional English
B. C. Dockery

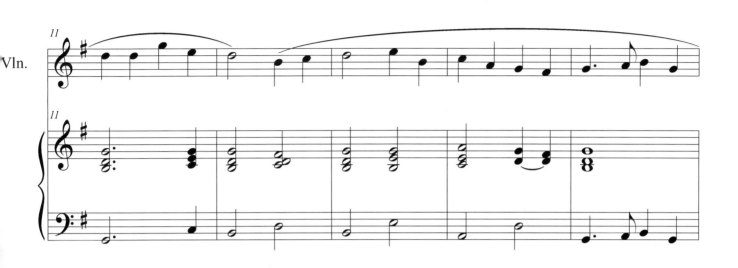

While Shepherds Watched Their Flock

Nahum Tate
B. C. Dockery

Made in United States
Orlando, FL
28 October 2024

53214772R00015